When Clocks Stop

Carmen Nappo

Crippled Beagle Publishing

Crippled Beagle Publishing, Knoxville, Tennessee
dyer.cbpublishing@gmail.com

Cover artwork by Carmen Nappo
Book design by Jody Dyer
Illustrations by Carmen Nappo

Cover image: NASA STS-127 crew [Public domain], via
Wikimedia Commons

Love section image: Wikimedia Commons contributors,
"File:Nils Sjögren Systrarna.JPG," *Wikimedia Commons, the free
media repository,*
https://commons.wikimedia.org/w/index.php?title=File:Nils_Sj
%C3%B6gren_Systrarna.JPG&oldid=331241539
(accessed March 26, 2019).

ISBN: 978-1-970037-15-9
Printed in the United States of America.

To the memory of Joan Parker MacReynolds.
My wife, my lover, my friend.

When Clocks Stop

When clocks stop
And time stands still
The spirit continues
And always will.

Poems

Life

It Could Have Been A Better Day

It could have been a better day
There could have been a better way
To say my regrets and sorrows
For these forgotten tomorrows.

A cell call going home
Will not do
There is so much more
Deserving of you.

In excuse I can find reason
Perhaps to satisfy
A missed birthday season
But work and worries
Cannot contend
The hurting of my dearest friend.

Our years together
Warrant behavior better
Far better than I have shown
And for this I ask your tolerance
And beg continued welcome
To your home.

Uppsala Autumn Afternoon

Under the sun
Waits the iguana.
In the heat it
Waits what will come
Beneath a burning sun.

Is this pleasure?
Is this the it?
How will I measure beneath a burning sun?

Alone I sit in a foreign land
With rock and blowing sand
Waiting, smoking a cigar.
Alone yet complete.
Beautiful women pass me buy
Too late—I have no eye.

Black is mostly.
And old songs remind
Me of my youth.
So far gone but not forgotten.

Why do they always take
Pleasure away?

Uppsala Sweden
12 October 2012

As I Recall My Transition Into Dotage

As I recall my transition into dotage
Was an easy one.
Unlike retirement or loss of a mate
Dotage required little to no adjustment.
In fact all that was required was my being
present.

Neither fear nor pain did I experience.
Not even shame.
  I found it warming to mess my
  underpants
  Now and then.
And when I could no longer use knife, fork, or
  spoon
A soda straw and a shake did quite well.

I did not forget my friends
Because I knew I once had them,
But now I can no longer distinguish
One from the other.
Thus, everybody is my friend.

There is not much I miss or regret.
I prefer to think I had a good live
And did many fine things
I prefer to think I had a happy life
With lots of parties and skipping children.

I prefer to think I was loved by a wonderful
person.

Or do I just wish that?

But either way there is no difference.
I still am, but not quite sure who that is.
I do recall a philosopher saying
Something about thinking and being,
But I'm not quite sure.

The transition into my dotage
Required accepting only one thing
Perpetual uncertainty.

Wageningen, Netherlands
Sunday, 27 March 2011

If I Could I Would

If I could I would
Write you a poem.
It would be a great poem
With words exotic and exact
It would tell you in ways
So much more meaningful
And memorable than simply
I care dearly for you.

If I could I would
Paint you a painting.
It would be a wonderful painting
With colors both vivid and subdued
With motions frozen in time
It would reveal to you my inner self
So that you could see
How much you are a part of me.

If I could I would
Write you a song.
It would be an enchanting song
With melody lyrical and lyrics musical
More rapturous than an angel's chorus
It would tell you how much
I want to be a part of your life.

But poet, painter, or composer I am not.
It is my lot
To possess no great devices or art
To express my feelings beyond the limits

Of my abilities.
I can only reach within my heart
Within its deepest part
And say I love you.

To Joan
13 October 2003

A Poet's Progress

Poetry was one before the others came.
Then a different music.
Another song follows.
This was so.

Put one word down
And another too quickly springs up
Making too much sense too quickly
The rejections pile too high
And before the song is over
It's ended.

Today a poem is too many
A million words sing the same
As another song follows.
The words form a silent harmony
    A gospel whispered on a surfboard,
    The testimony of a Bronx cheer.

Try another tune
Try FORTRAN IV or V
Or IBM Assembler
Each binary bit a subtle nuance
Every punched card
A quatrain in iambic hexadecimal
Rejection slips by Univac.
Tomorrow's poem.
Frantic fingers dodge a cappella.

Words whoosh by in search of flowers.
Images of morning garbage
Restful as a shattered mirror.
The media is the message
But there's nothing left to say.

No more rejection slips
Just 'Return to Sender.'

I Can Live In A World Of Speculation

I can live in a world of speculation
And dance on the heads of pins
Or I can believe that I know something
Or I know that I can believe something
For nowhere is certain and
Everywhere is meaningless.

Above a stormy sky
There lies glorious Summer
And I can jest
At winter's discontent.

I'm on a merry-go-round
Going left to right and right to left
Yet I move only forward.
Tricks of the eye and of the mind
Arrest and cloak me from the world
And the world I would pursue.

As a child I believed in a child's God
But that God abandoned me.
In time, I was condemned to be
And to be alone.

Now each year grows shorter than the last
And I can see well the obscurity of the past.
Truth I know now is what I make It
Just as a child on a pretty path home
I made a perfect world.

If Witches Wished

If witches wished,
Which witches wish
Which witch's wish
Wished witches wished?

January 2011

When Life Fails

When life fails the last test
Then dim the lights and go to rest.

Now is where the dreams are real
And empty is all we feel.

Come my brother I'll take you where
Sunsets last forever and forever still the air.

Neither end nor beginning
And time is a memory
Where shadows walk the paths of history

When life fails
We as the rest
Continue to the next test.

I Wish I Were A Pirate

I wish I were a pirate
So I could say, "Avast!" and "Arrrrrrrrr!"
And wave me musket
A'swinging on a halyard
With cutlass on a lanyard
Lashed about me waist.
Arrrrrrrrr!

Aye, thems would be the days,
Winds a'plenty; fair the sky
And great plunder for all.

Truth,
But them days are none.

Still,
I wish I were a pirate
And me home the emerald sea
With Davy Jones' locker fathoms below.
Worries be me ballast
And anchor be me dole.

Oh, and aye,
Nay a'this or that
I'll let befoul me way.
And on me fair corsair.
No Jonahs jinx the air .
Me crew!

Good lads all, dancing pretty
To drum and fife
While old dogs
With grog and pipe
Spin yarns
Of a younger life.

But alas, naught will be.
No pirate's life for me.
Only fancy dreams
To dally
Of a life upon the sea.

13 June 2014

When I Was A Child

When I was a child
I dreamt of toys and tales
Of cowboys and whales
Of ships with red sails
And sand in sand pails.

When I was a child
I made a garden by the house
Not much bigger than a mouse
I would make balls bounce
I watched a cat prepare to pounce.

When I was a child
Dragons would fly
With clouds of fire throughout the sky
And when they vanished I wondered why
They never ever said goodbye.

It's The Little Hurts That Hurt The Worst

It's the little hurts that hurt the worst.
The absent thank-you
The missed touch or retarded smile.
Each a cracker crumb placed atop another
Until it cannot stand
And crashes in an avalanche of neglect
Burying what love and kindness remained.

Big hurts ask big forgiveness
A penance and a promise
A dinner and a film
Or perhaps a new car.
Big hurt can be bought.

But little hurts go unchecked
A confused meaning, a mistaken word
A gaze beyond a shoulder
We note and not remember
Or forget before realized.

Crackers in bed seem innocent enough
Until it's dark yet awake we lie
And wonder why we itch so
For no apparent reason.

Then sleepy morning dawns ill-humored.
Deaf to sunrise and kitty's attentions.
Then we forget to smile or wait a while

To hear Granny's stories one more time.
And in the end, the end of the day
We say it was a dreary day
And take more crackers to bed.

The little hurts accrue unnoticed or ignored.
Paper cuts or flea bites on a dog.
It's when we lose an arm or down a dog
We seek reason instead of sensitivity.
Beds were made for love and sleep
But not for crackers.

2 May 2005

The Wind

The wind is blowing the leaves around
The stillness I remember now
Was never really there
But only in a dream.

The leaves before the wind
In silence fell
From the tree I shook.
In neat piles to burn
I raked them.

But the leaves
Where only shades of leaves
Of an autumn dreaming
In a clam beyond the memory
Without the wind
That was never really there.

Genealogy

Do I let them fall between my fingers
Or collect the pieces and make
A mosaic incomplete and uncommon?

Voids pervade this fabric
Covering in gossamer what we call a life.
Shadows dwell in semi-darkness
As I wonder through this fog of time.

Now faces stare blank in crinkled
photographs
And blurred words confuse yellowed pages.
What once breathed and loved and danced
Lies buried beneath a dust of lost
remembrances.

Who knew once these faces?
Who heard once a spoken name?
How do I join the pieces?
Where ends history and what of fancy?

If my yesterdays are dreams
Then what of the days before my time?
Is there sense to these constructions,
Or is the meaning only in the doing?

8 July 2003

Love

I Have Two Daughters
dedicated to Cora and Heather

I have two daughters
Though both are grown women
They remain my girls.

One lives in a world of art and opinion
One lives in a world real and defined
Both love me in their ways
As I love them.

I thought we would be friends
But parents make poor friends.
It's a question of control.

Raising children is like
Throwing away a boomerang.
They always are your children.

Before they became women
I was bonded to them
But then
Quite suddenly
I was out of the circle
And I went rogue.

Now the boomerang
Has returned
And they are raising me.
I'm in good hands.

18 December 2018

Moon Upon The Water

Moon upon the water
The night is still
A breeze disturbs the water
The moon is gone.

The morning is begun
Before the rising of the sun
Each to their own
Fields to be sown.

Sun upon the water
The day is busy
A breeze disturbs the water
The sun is gone.

The night is begun
We are home
Jasmine fills the air
This is love.

Saturday, 22 October 2005

What Is The Distance Between Loving and Caring?

What is the distance between loving and
caring?
Is it so small as to be unnoticed?
Is it so vast as to be unseeable?
Where does one end and the other begin?

We fall in love
But grow to care
Nor are they the same thing
Else why the two words?

The young fall in love
And the old grow to care
Young love will fade
But caring can only increase

Therein lies the distance
Between loving and caring
It is a string of time
A lifetime long.

ᴸᵛe Is Singular
a poem for Joan

My love is singular
Constant, eternal, omnipresent
Day after day
Through years before and after
Changing clothes like paper dolls
Upside down or spun around
She is.
Always was and will be
Unchanged.

In the center of her being is a Being
I can neither see nor touch.
More tenuous than vapor
More solid than a neutron star
A wormhole to God
A doorway to impossibility
Yet all I can see are ripples in an ocean
Fringe patters of a solar eclipse.

In some far distant place
Perhaps an uncounted galaxy
Signals emerge hoping to be heard
Thus does she reach out to the universe
Saying "I am here. I am."
Do I hear her? Do I? Really?

She has, had, and will have many names
But at this time I know only a few
A blind man touching the base of Everest
Would know as much.
Words in a vacuum say as much.

I want to know her.
I want to know her name.
I want to touch that spark of life.
I want as much as I can get.

My love is singular.
There is no other.
There never will be.

Boulder, Colorado
7 February 2009

I Will Open Myself To Beauty
a poem for my wife Joan

I will open myself to beauty
Arms reaching I will embrace it
Caress it
Taste its colors
      Green and orange and scarlet and cobalt
And see again yesterday's promise
Fulfilled and redeemed.

I will give myself to beauty
Surrender to its inevitable essence
Its essential existence
And these will be mine as I am theirs
For beyond there is only nothingness.

Worlds join at beauty.
Each has its own.
Maybe different, maybe not
But always unchanging
Always there
Maybe seen, maybe not.

Our worlds touch at beauty
Speaking with silence
      Haystacks in purple twilight
      Sipping coffee at late-night dinners
Motion in stillness
      Even galaxies madly whirl

Ballet burned in the memory
Darkness with light
Sense in nonsense
All transcendent in beauty.

This is the center of my being
This is you and me and a cat
This is cosmic and unending
This is beauty.

Boulder, Colorado
8 February 2009

Love Is A Garden

Love is a garden of flowers
Alive with bees and color
And darting hummingbirds,
All forming a moment
That can last a lifetime.

It is not the planting
That makes a garden
Nor dreams within
A seed catalog.

It is not in the planning.
Anticipation plays no part.
It is not the size.
A pond is not necessary.

The garden, like love,
Thrives only through the
Constant hands of the gardener.
It requires constant care.
It lives within the gardener,
And it dies from neglect.

Love cannot be planted
And forgotten.
Each day must it be tended
With strong and gentle hands.
Love given to a garden

Returns in times of blooms
And remains in winter's snow
Preparing for the coming spring.

A garden is a promise,
A trust to be kept,
A dedication,
A knowing.

Love, like a garden,
When kept with love,
Will last forever.

She Walks With Grace And High Appointment
my first poem for Joan

She walks with grace and high appointment
Head neither up nor aside
Nor does she hide
Or show her beauty.
Hers is not the face
Of a face
That is looked at.

Eyes fixed and away
With naked feet she glides
Across Elysian Fields.
Unending searching between
Heaven and hell
Unending helping between
Heaven and hell.

She is of one purpose,
Which is every purpose.
She has no boundaries and thus
Is never out of bounds.
Her clocks tick at her will.
She is the sorceress of her universe.
And there she spins
A universe of unlimited realities.
There one can spend
Eternal summer with ice cream

And baseball games and
Music under a tent.

There one can journey
Into age and death
Without despair or fear
And pass with dignity and love
From here to there.

She walks with grace and high appointment
Disturbing all yet touching not even a leaf.
She is an energy beyond science.
She is motion without work.
She is direction without destination.
She is mystery.
She is inevitable.

30 August 2003

When I Fell In Love With You

Dear Joan,

I've wanted to tell you this for some time, and now is the time. I want to tell you when I fell in love with you. It was, I believe, spring 1994.

You took me on a hike in the Smoky Mountains. I spent the previous night with you, and we left in the morning. I can't remember the name of the trail, but it was a fun walk of a mile or so up to a cave. We crossed some streams along the way, and there were other people on the trail as well. We brought our lunches (you made them), and we ate there. It was a beautiful morning. And I was excited to be with you.

We left shortly after lunch; the place was getting crowded. Just before we got to the parking lot, I started telling you a joke about silent gas emissions. When we got to the parking lot, I told you the punch line, which was the doctor saying, "Well, the first thing we need to do is check your hearing." You started laughing uncontrollably. You were crying and howling at the same time. A woman passed us and said, "Wow, that must have been funny." Really! She said that.

Of course you don't remember, because you were crazy with laughter. That is when I fell in love with you. How could I resist that passion, that exuberance, that love of fun? I had never before seen such abandon in a woman. That is when I fell in love with you, and that love continues to grow.

All my love,
Carmen

All That Is Good In Me
to Joan on our 12ᵗʰ anniversary

All that is good in me
Is your good
All the light that is in me
Is your light
All the love that is in me
Is your love
All that is joyful in me
Is your joy

You have given me so much
You have given me so much of your life
You have led me to a greater life
Than I ever imagined.

All of my happiness
Is your happiness
All of my peace
Is your peace
All of me
Is in you

1 January 2012

You Have Given Me A Gift

You have given me a gift
More precious than gold
More beautiful than jewels
More valuable than light in darkness
More comforting than water to thirst
      And rest to weariness.
You have given me what I lost
What I thought irredeemable.
You have stopped the clock
Counting remaining moments.
You have given form to mist
      And shape almost forgotten.
You have defined a new word
Given meaning to absurd.
Stopped the bleeding
With an infusion of hope
A life's renaissance
      The beginning of a future.
No longer adrift in dreams
I perinate with purpose into
A world of possibility.
Fresh scenes never before seen
The tastes of color
      And the scents of magic.
You have given me my life.

Friday, 13 July 2018

Friends

Poem For Kathryn

Ever seeking the unasked question
This daughter of Eliot
Wonders about in time
And in time she will find her balance.

Ever forward she faces
An uncertain future, yet unafraid.

Hers is not an easy task.
To make a whole life
From parts of lives
Is neither simple nor satisfying,
Yet she has no choice.

Sometimes the whole is less than
The sum of its parts,
And this is especially true
When lovers unwillingly leave us.

Still, she survives,
Battered and beautiful.
A hero brave and true
Continues her search.

Hers is not "A world of speculation."
"What might have been" didn't.
"What has been" did.
There will be a tomorrow
And Kathryn will be there.

22 August 2003

A Man Remembered
for Bill Martin

He will not carry the wind
Nor wail at the end of days.
A man of strength and pride
Who honors debts and pays
With bitter-sweet smile
Charon's crossing fee.

The man is free. Released.
His spirit is the wind
That blows the ashes to ashes.
His dust makes red the setting sun
And for that we know him.

His voice could boom as morning thunder,
Yet gentle, disturbing not a butterfly.
In youth he was a running man.
In wisdom he knew us all well.

To be unique is never to see another.
We shall not wait for your return.
We shall remember your days
And be again together
As ghosts in another time.

Dear Bill, you will be missed.

Life is a Ride Far Better Than Any Other

Effortless motion is the thrill, joy, and pleasure of a ride. Whatever form it takes, from a dog sled to the space shuttle, a ride is almost always fun.

Do you not, deep inside, still long to be Carried by your father or rocked by your Mother?

We love rides.

Now it's your birthday, but I don't know your age, and so I'll say it this way:

When next you are asked your age, say, "I've had the thrill, joy, and pleasure of riding on the Earth XX-times around the Sun. It is a really great ride."

Happy Birthday, Denise, and keep on riding.

John And Colene

Two worlds stand together
Each alone, unique, and center seeking.
Neither needs the other.
Thus, like gravity, they are kept together
By forces only imagined.

Such a system, these two spinning worlds,
Cannot argue the good or bad of it,
Nor can they feel 'must'.
There need be only surrender
To what we call love.

These worlds are kept together
By forces only imagined.
Neither science by wit
Nor art by whimsey
Can understand love.

Love like gravity
Holds together worlds
Spinning intertwined yet apart.
Love is inexorable.
The genius of a couple is that
They know this.

Colene

The paths most follow are seldom their own
Pointless it seems they wander and roam
Yet some of us choose and make our own way
And live life in full each day to day.

Such a one is you Colene
For you are more,
Much more, than you seem.

With deep affection,
Carmen

Going To The East
a poem for Salma

Going to the east
Will take you to the west
Thus east and west are one
On the same sides of the circle.

When up becomes down
And day becomes night
When wrong becomes right
And fear becomes might
Then balance is achieved
And at its center lies
Delight.

Live with peace and love
Salma
Insha'Alla

Stockholm, Sweden
3o November 2011

All Life Is History

All life is history
And all history is time.

From the first creepy-crawlies
To the red sands of Mars,
History has lived and shall
Continue unto nothingness.

History is all we can see
And even that is unclear.
We must learn history
And imagine the truth.

Yet we pass through history
As easily as neutrinos
Pass through rocks,
And of the billions per second,
Only a few are counted.

So few of us detect history,
Appreciate its omnipresence,
Know its beauty and life.

Rare is the fine wine
And rare is Tom Fine.

Good Things Do Not Last
for my wife Joan on our 14th anniversary

Good things do not last.
They break as easily as a hummingbird's egg
The finest crystal can outlast a good thing

A good thing can be broken by a wayward
glance,
A whisper, a lie, betrayal.
Nor is a good thing love.
Lovers can be un-good to each other.

Good things will fade and wither with time.
Good things can be as easily forgotten
As those who made them.

A good thing must always be refreshed.
A good thing endures
By a kiss, a smile, a touch, a caring,
A not forgetting.

Love, too, can be a good thing
If it is attended and loved.

My wife, my Joan
Is a good thing
And I will tender her
And I will love her
So that this good thing shall
Last as long as I.

She Passes Through The Door Lightly
a poem for Gerda Osborne

She passes through the door lightly
As gossamer in an April lilac breeze.
She was here, and now she plays there
On the other side of life
While we wait in memories
Looking forward to a promise
Of yet another time.

Is she hiding in a play house,
Playing tricks as girls do?
Can she see us as clearly
As we see her?
Can she touch us? Can we touch her?

She passes through the door
And it is a very thin door.
So thin it can't be measured,
Yet if it could, would the measure
Be moments?

I am not sad.
She had many days
Upon the soft grass
Among us laughing children.

Now the days are over,
And she is home.
Oh, the wonder of it all.

I Cannot Escape My World

I cannot escape my world
For I am in it.
And yet I seek the peace of silence.
The Nothingness.

At the beginning Nothingness
Became time and space
A condition of unchanging
Particles and numbers.

Since the beginning nothing has been created.
The Cosmos is a momentary arrangement of
Space and time with neither direction nor
purpose
And some call this Reality.

But this is Existence, not Essence.
And Essence transcends
The motions of particles
And the summing of numbers
For these are actions only.
These are things we do.

Essence does not change
It does not do things.
For a while it assumes
A state we call Life

And then returns to Nothingness
And Nothingness
Is the only Reality.

I cannot escape my world
For I am in it.
But what I am, My Essence,
Is not of this world
But is Nothingness.

A poem for Salma Light
29 May 2015

Eighty Days In June
a birthday card for Colene

Eighty days in June.
"Not so," you say,
But June's in spring
And spring's a thing
Eternal.

Eighty seconds, days, or years
Have no meaning in a world of
Always.

'Always' is eternal.
Eternal as youth.
And youth is a thing
In spring.

We find ourselves
On a fair Saturday evening
In June with fireflies
Floating in flowers.

Forever to remember
Colene in revealing navy blue.
Eighty seconds, days or years
In an unchanging youth
That is You.

19 June 2017

Relative To Time These Years Are Tiny
a poem written for John McCord in celebration of his 60th anniversary

Relative to time these years are tiny.
Bits of dust untouched within the hour's glass
A molecule of mist within the fog
Remarkable only in its similarity.

Yet these bits of clay and passing moments
Are neither alone nor unnoticed but travel
With us toward an unseen goal
And are remembered by many forgotten.

Along this way we pass from wild youth
To white-haired wisdom and weathered
babushkas.
Unredeemable, our knowledge lies in quiet
repose
Beneath our hand-made quilts
Before our home fires
While always within our hearts
We know that we know.

No school but life prepares us for this day.
With silver eyes we see the distant way
And blessed are those happy few
Who own their road and love its view.

Knoxville, Tennessee
Sunday, 11 January 2009

Living On The Brink
a poem for Frankie Hulett

It must be maddening living on the brink.
One foot on a cliff's edge the other on air,
Never certain in a world that should be.
Surrounded by unmanageable possibilities,
Yet she manages to step with grace
From one day to another.

It must be sad never being sure
Of what and when and why.
So many problems to face and fix
And yet she looks for more.
For there is so much that is wrong
She feels could be right.

She remains neither mad nor sad
But continues resolute and determined.
This is the source of her strength.
For she knows above all
That she is and will be.
Existence is her essence.

One sees the child in her smile,
A pretty girl in a pretty new dress.
While she has known pain and loss
And loneliness,
That child remains undimmed.

She seldom looks behind
Because she knows that country.
All that matters is what's ahead
And how best to get there.
And when she arrives
She will be known.

Things Are Seldom As They Are
a poem for Ann Exum

Things are seldom as they are.
Words change from mouth to ear,
And tricks of light and shadow
Betray our visions of reality.

What lies still and quiet
Dances and sings before our eyes.
Who has come and gone
Remains ever with us.

Pain is the price of living
And most painful is the passing
Of a mother's child.

But pain is a temporary thing.
And while it is remembered,
So is its cause.
And that brings us full circle
To a life's beginning
For giving birth is also painful.

Things are seldom as they are.

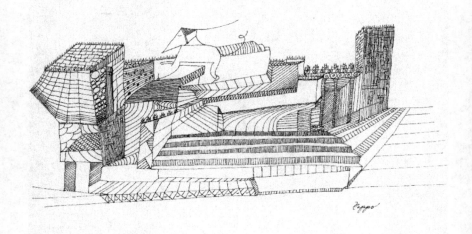

Time

Where Have They Gone

I

The rain drops fell upon the quiet,
Small and ringing sounds
About the stillness of those days
Moist with dew upon the young grass
Wildly running, growing without care
Into the vastness
Felt so seldom by the young things.

Echoes then were fun to hear
Among the Castle walls
Before they turned to cold hard stone
And we, grown up, become afraid
Afraid of echoes,
And those that make them.

Back again to the day before we knew.
Back again.

And there stillness rings
The soundless hum we heard
Alone upon the voiceless grass,
And we wondered why.

And the light shown
Brightly in a darkness long ago
We sought the one there unafraid
And wondered who.
But now the rain falls
Heavy upon the frozen echoes,

Speaking only with the earth
Unheard beside the crumbled Castle walls.

II

I heard it yesterday within the pond,
Together swimming ducks
Took my offerings speaking,
But not to me.

And the leaves lie
Upon the ground
Before me dying
Quietly as they must.
For a moment
Passed faintly a whisper
From forgotten walls
But I did not listen.

And soon the vastness
Shrinks to that which was before
Our knowing that it would
So quickly disappear.

And as all the drops and echoes
Fade with the grass and dying leaves
In an Autumn darkness
Yet light enough to see two Mallards fly away,
I cannot bid them farewell.

Seattle, Washington Spring 1968

The End of Words

The end of words.
It slams shut the door
Against a meaningless time
Sending echoes of thought
Crashing around my now
Isolated and empty mind.

The End of words.
Vast clouds of probability swept away,
Entropy is maximized
And endless possibility destroyed.
I can no longer speak.

Now lies a realm
Unseen but for a few,
And I once knew their names,
But now the silence is profound.
Everywhere is nothing.
There is no focus.
I can stand on my head
And the world remains unchanged.

A Universe without grammar
Remains forever unseen, unknown.
Wills struggle for illusion.
Time is a clock.
Tomorrow is eternal.
And the moment is ignored.

The End of words
Marks not the end of life.
No, nothing that simple.
The end of words
Marks the end of existence.

25 September 25 2003

Being Young

Being young is always Becoming
Being young is knowing Forever
Being young is owning no Yesterdays
Being young is seeing only with Eyes
Being young is living without Years
Being young is being Happy

21 January 2004

How Can I Judge Tomorrow?

How can I judge tomorrow?
How can I judge yesterday?
In my world neither is real
One a shadow the other a fantasy
Both specious and irrelevant
    Powerless and impotent
    Empty and vacant
And yet I spend my days
In either realm
Anticipating and regretting.

How can I judge
What can't be marked?
Each tomorrow is a snowflake
In a blizzard of probability,
And what is true
Is only by chance.

How can I judge
What is singular?
If there exists but a single flower,
Is it a good flower?
There is always but a single yesterday
Which is incomparable and unredeemable.

I wonder on a plane of time
Forever now
But not forever,

My mind in vain
Tries to right the clock
To a fond yesterday
And a fair tomorrow.

But if I judge not yesterday,
Then perhaps tomorrow
May not judge me,
And in that state of grace
I could lovingly let it be.

30 December 2004

A Little Girl Skipping
a poem for Mona Wilson on the passing of her mother

A little girl skipping
In shiny new shoes,
Silken hair dancing
Above shiny new eyes,
Unaware of the world
And the ever-present hand.

The hand that combed her hair
And dried her tears,
That hand was always there
To push aside her fears.

That hand would never let go.
It's presence she would always know.
Even when apart,
That hand was on her heart.

With time she watched
That hand grow old.
Then it was she who
Now took hold
To guide her in
The twilight years
And help arrest
The darkening fears.

Full circle now these hands have come,
The first to touch the first to feel
The last to touch that which was real.
And in that moment, all moments past
Remain so touched until the last.

1 May 2005

Where Did They Begin?

Where did they begin?
These pointless words
These vacant concepts.
An idiot's tale
Full of woe and sadness
All forgiven by a simple,
"I'm sorry. It was a mistake."

Yesterday is not redeemable.
What is indelible
Cannot be changed
And the shock of being wrong
Does not make it right.
There are no mistakes.
There are only choices.

I know my sins.
I've watched them grow
From seed to flower
Within days or years
Each step by choice
And not by chance.

Mistakes are found and caught.
They are discovered.
They are never loved.

We do not hide correctness
Because we accept it
As being good.

Mistakes are sins
We chose to make
And every action has a stake.
If I pick 7 but the number's 10
Then the mistake is in the choosing.
But if I pick 10
Then I have won
For fortune is not in getting caught.

Sunday, 16 October 2005

We Are But Moments
to my wife Joan on our 11th anniversary

We are but moments
In an infinity of time
But no matter how long
We live
Moments will be all
We have.

And these moments
I spend with you
Will be sweet and warm
Knowing that you cared
And loved me.
What more could I ask?

31 December 2010

Time Is The Avatar Of Death

Time is the avatar of death.
It is the ultimate end of everything.
Waiting, inexorable,
Infinitely patient,
Omnipresent and omnipotent
Eternal Summer.

Oh God,
Protect me from time's wrath.
Shelter me.
Preserve me.

Yet even God
Succumbs.

11 July 2011

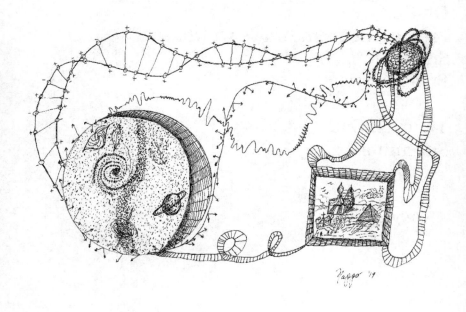

Essence

Simple Prayer

For all the souls
    Both young and old
For all the lives
    Both bought and sold
For all the tears
    Both hot and cold
For all the years
    We try to hold
We give our love
    And thereby
        Love behold.

Phoenix, Arizona
27 September 2001, in memory of 9 September.

I Heard The Owl Call My Name

I heard the owl call my name*
And while the people slept
Moonbeams searched
And found me looking
Through an open window.
>   Then I heard the owl call my name
>   And I knew.

I heard the owl call my name
Clearly yet far away
So very far away
Even before the earth
Touched my feet
>   The owl called my name.
>   And I knew.

Have others heard the owl?
Would they know my name?
But the others sleep
In dreams of sleep
With little time for day.
>   The owl called my name
>   And only I heard.

As a child I remember
Being hungry at play
And anxious for dinner
Yet wanting not to leave

I heard then my mother softly call my name
    A sound as ever knowing and loving as
    the owl's.
Oh, how happy I felt running home.

20 November 2004

'In the Alaskan Indians' culture, it is believed that
when one hears an owl call his name then it is time to
die.

In My Heart I Am An Honorable Man.

In my heart I am an honorable man
I want to be caring and loving
Because these I was denied
And I have found that
Love is the only path to happiness.

Feelings are painful for me to bear
And I am by nature sensitive.
When I see another in fear
I feel that fear and its desperation
My stomach wrenches, and I want to flee.

In my heart I am a sinful man.
I don't want to be, but I am.
I was not born that way.
I became that way,
But it was not my choice.

My sensitivity attracts needy women
And in turn so am I attracted to that need.
I will be happy if I can make her happy.
That is all I ever wanted to do.
If she is happy and without fear
Then I am at peace.

But this peace is illusion.
I cannot make another happy.
Filling the needs of the needy

Is neither heroic nor romantic.
It is only self-serving.

In my heart I am a fearful man.
My life has been
A walk on spring-time ice.
Each step, each year,
Trembling from one to the other,
Never knowing when or where.

My father killed my soul
And I hated him for that.
But self-pity is just that.
I am a fearful man
Yet still a man.
I can redeem myself.
I can atone.
But how?
How much pain does it take?
And what of tomorrow?

In my heart I am a lying man.
If I knew the truth,
I would say it.
But I don't.

I believed that what was mine
Was mine.

Now I know that is wrong.
Truly what is mine is ours,
But still I want mine!

In my heart I am a shameful man.
In the street I learned of sex,
And it was naughty and dirty
Something done in hiding
With lust and fear.

It is so compelling!
Not an addiction
But an analgesic.
I have lived so much of my life
Doing wrong.
How could I avoid the guilt?

Pride and conceit
See only me,
And yet it is you
Who is truly wronged,
And I am so sorry for that.

In my heart I am a lonely man.
Inside the walls I've built in defense.
Was I only five
When I learned
That I was safe only when alone?

I am doing all I can do,
Which is the best I can do,
But is that enough?
Is it still too rough?

A path we have engaged.

In my heart I am an honorable man.
Of this I like to think,
But this is smoke and magic,
A cheap trick I read in a book.
The truth is
I am only a man.

Wednesday, 3 August 2005

Altruism Was Beaten Into Me

Altruism was beaten into me
By anonymous philanthropists,
And unknown politicians who
Seduced me into self-sacrifice.
Heroically, I threw away my limbs
Believing the world is safer for it.

I have and have been killed countless times
All in the name of God or fatherland.
My mother beat her breasts
While my father proudly marched,
Holding a photograph of me once alive.

I was always too young to know
The difference between life and duty.
Questions and doubts were bad.
They cut me out from the rest,
And I was afraid of being alone.

Nothing is more destructive than an idea
Unless it is the truth.
Honor, I've been told, is the only reality
And partially blown-up men
Are more desirable than whole ones.

I have been told this by those who know
better.
I know this because they told me so.

My teachers asked me only questions
To which they knew the answers,
And I was ashamed of appearing to be smart.

Now I march from here to there,
Hoping to be wounded but without pain.
And then the world will know how good I
      was,
And I will be loved all the more.
I know this because I was told this
By those who know more than I.

Tuesday, 13 December 2005

So Many Roads
a poem of reunion

So many roads
So many lost upon their ways,
Yet we remain and continue,
Never knowing our journey's end,
Nor do we worry or pretend.

The many years
Seen in a blink,
And time itself
Is what we think.

These precious seconds
Here and now
Will remain
And life will continue.

21 August 2015

The Acropolis

The will to bring home the wreckage
And put it up again
The way it was before
Is gone.

I spend a day in searching
Thoughts from Princeton to Seattle.
We could not find
The ways to Greece
And spent our youth
On nameless roads.

Yet even now
The hill grows smaller
Than three thousand years ago.
Each pilgrim takes a tiny piece
And tries to put it up again
To find the answer in the rubble.

So great a circle is thirty years
To have come so far
And to have never found Greece.
And Christ still lies
In chips of shattered mirrors.
For resurrection cannot endure
So many fragments of truth.

These are the ways it is now,
For without Greece or Christ,

Remains only time and motion
And searching for tomorrow
In the wreckage of monuments.

Redeem Me Lord

Redeem me Lord.
I am so tired.
My sorrows are plenty
My joys so few.

In a dark place
I wander blind
Searching a doorway
To your loving grace.

Redeem me Lord
Take away this endless yellow August,
This endless cruel winter.
Place me gently in an empty meadow.

Quiet.
Oh so
Very quiet.

I have never hurt you Lord.
I have never hurt anyone.

I have no recompense.
I have nothing.

Redeem me Lord.
I am so tired.
My nights are plenty.

My days so few.
So little known.
So little new.

1 August 2016

The True Artist

The true artist
Brushes not with paint
Or writes with poems
Nor colors dreams
Of fading scenes
Of a moment's beauty.

The true artist
Makes no music, dance, or tragedy,
No prophesy entombed in stone.
The true artist does not stand alone
Above humanity.

The artist,
The true artist,
Does none of these,
For art is not in its doing
But in its being.

Art
Though some may call it living,
Others may call it prayer.

Meditations On Truth

1. Nothing is more transparent than truth.

2. Truth is an act of consciousness.

3. Truth exist neither in nature nor science.

On A Hill We Missed It

A scarlet haze surrounded an adventurer
Of self-conceived virtue,
Itself the greater ecstasy,
    An ending to desire.
Unheard, not listened to,
Dejected in the desert, searching.
But fantasies still torment the flesh
Too long denied.

It escaped you then
And now—the same fear.
It's too late.
They hung you up.

Eyes unfeeling, words unreaching,
No pity, they wait you thus.
Transfixed by blood and terror
Arms of wood and nails begin
To tremble in the final agony
But still the same fear.

And then it comes
And goes so quickly
And all the knowledge of it
Passes with you.

It is done.
It is ended.

History Is Humanity

Humanity is history
And to know history
Is to know what we are.

"How did I get here?"
Asked a man to a woman.
"How did I get here?"
Asked a photon to a neutrino.

Is it history?
Is it science?
Each contains the other
Like electromagnetism.

Regardless of your dimension,
Cause must proceed effect.
And things move through spacetime
Along as many paths
As there are dimensions.

But they all move
Along a single path
In the mind of God.

Death

California

A poem of life and wandering and the
sadness of its ending.
Alone and unattended and waiting in the
shadows
Amid the illusions of men long since dead or
dying
And unfulfilled and wanting to have had a
meaning.

Too long and too far away
Our eyes grew faint in searching
And the years in wanting gave way to vanity
And fantasies of other worlds led us often
astray.

Yet always, faintly, beyond the seeing
Whispered a memory
Of a warmer sun burning without haste
And living things and dying things would
Pass naturally from one to the other.

But now it is too late.
In the end the last to find is time,
And we the dead
Now know the mystery of and the promise in
The last light's dying.

Alone we wait the coming of the silent sleep
And the final act
While quietly the unknowing children leave us
As they must, to search for California.

1959

A Poem For The Dead And The Dying

I have tried to plot
The difference between the dead and the
dying,
But instead of a curve
I find only a single point.

In a world of endless possibilities,
In a universe of infinite chance,
All nature and time
Can be reduced to a single point.

Thus, in this place and in this time
Exists all that was and will be.
It lies at a single point
In the center of our being.

We are neither dead nor dying
But rather both.
We may think we are alive,
But how is that different?

Though our parents are dead
They live within us.
A live rose and a dead rose
Are both roses.

Nothing ends that had not a beginning.

If time is a point it neither separates nor
distinguishes.
We can count the seconds or the stars
But how is that meaningful?

Life is neither flesh nor spirit,
Nor motion or stillness,
Nor mass or energy,
Nor man or God.

Life is this moment
Which contains All.

5 May 2005

We Must Succumb

We must succumb
To the muffled drum
In cadence slow
With eyes cast low
The caissons bear
The lives we share
And the battle is won
When day is done.

Role the drum
A mournful hum
And still the fife
Against a life
For children cry
When fathers dye
And mothers weep
While children sleep.

March we thus
From dawn to dusk
So many boys have died.
Dark's the sky
And heaven knows why
All the Generals lied.

Sleep my brother
Sleep as no other

For waken you shall not.
With terrible heart
You did your part
And died here on this spot.

We must succumb
To the muffled drum
Compelled to stay
Until the day
When days all end
And to hell descend
Tattoo, tattoo, the last to do.
Tattoo, tattoo, tattoo.

15 June 2005

A Year Without Spring

The previous spring
Being an ordinary spring
Was not especially memorable.

We didn't know
It was our last spring.

Our future ended
At the beginning of summer
When we learned that
This would be our last summer.

In August we found
Ourselves in a new life
Within a world shrinking
Of interest except for
Each other and the ones
We loved.

And of course the eclipse,
Observed from earth's embrace
Because you were too week to
Sit or stand.
Still you marveled at God's beauty.

As September waned
So did your waking hours.

On All Saints Day
We celebrated your 80th year
Surrounding you on our bed.
And a few times
We waited quietly while you dozed.

Thanksgiving with my daughters,
The bedroom lit by a tiny electric tree,
We laughed and enjoyed our
Cracker Barrel turkey dinners.

Thus began the last sixteen days
Of your wonderful life
A life of curiosity, creativity, love, pain, and
kindness.

If I had known how much you loved me,
I would have learned how much I loved you.

19 December 2017

At The End Of The Day

At the end of the day
And the book is closed
Who's left to remember
What and where and when.
And recalling
And another sigh
I see the unending cycle
Not dying
But starting anew.

I reach for the phone
Alone
For you're not there.
You're not at home.

My heart hurts.
I'm lonely
And I cry
A cry that grows
To anger.

There is none to ask
But only myself
And I answer the only answer.

Without death
There was no life.

July 2018

Carmen Nappo is a retired research meteorologist who specialized in air quality and atmospheric turbulence. Has been writing poetry on and off for over 60 years. Inspiration comes to him in the form of a phrase or a play on words with which he weaves a thought or a moment. Nappo does not consider himself a poet but rather a translator from imagination into reality.

CPSIA information can be obtained
at www.ICGtesting.com
Printed in the USA
BVHW070725300619
552281BV00003B/364/P